MANAGING STRESS

A girlfriend-to-girlfriend handbook for parenting children with ADHD, Asperger's, SPD & more ...

Robin Bartko

Dedicated to all the girlfriends who have children with challenges, and to my beautiful son who has taught me so much about unconditional love, compassion and life.

CONTENTS

PREFACE

My Story

If you are reading this book then you either have a child with challenges, are the friend or family member of someone who does or are an educator. You are probably searching for help. If so, I know where you are because I was there myself.

My name is Robin Bartko. The bulk of my real-life, girlfriend experience comes from two places: raising my adoptive son, Noah, and providing adoption support and education for many years.

When we adopted my son from overseas, he was 21 months old. He was almost bald, a little chunky and had big blue eyes. He was really adorable! One of the doctors that cleared him for travel called him "Little Buddha." After traveling halfway around the world (literally) we came home and got him settled into our home. From the start, I noticed that his behaviors were often different than my two older children. When he colored pictures, they were totally illegible. He was easily distracted, didn't like loud noises or the wind, and his eyes tended to sometimes look sideways. He also liked to line up his toys. Also, he came home with some minor medical issues which affected his gut health. The interesting thing was that, despite these unusual behaviors, my son picked up on language very easily. He also could memorize things fairly well and would repeat them often. There were pockets of inconsistencies that I noticed as soon as we adopted him that I couldn't explain.

Some time passed and I went to my local school system to get my son evaluated. I thought that perhaps he had some developmental delays. The school system did a short battery of tests including checking his eyes, hearing, and performance on some development tasks. The school system indicated that all these tests checked out OK and inferred that "boys will be boys." However, in my heart, I knew that my son's behaviors were more than "boys will be boys" and I insisted on getting him services.

It has been a long journey raising my son. We have made some tremendous progress and have had some setbacks. One of the more surprising things to me has been how hard it has been at times to get him services. There have been many therapies that we have tried – some worked, and some did not. Overseeing his schooling has been a full-time plus job.

It has often been a lonely task of raising my son. Many parents of typical children just don't understand the demands on those of us who are parents of children with challenges. I have been blessed to have contacts in the adoption community who have given me advice and shared their joys and struggles in raising their children with challenges.

A few years after adopting my son, my husband and I started an adoption website to promote adoption and help other parents. We had this adoption site for over 10 years. We would get calls from people all over the United States considering adoption, but many of the calls and contacts were from post adoptive parents who were seeking guidance with raising their child. I became a parent mentor and connected these parents with other parents that had children with similar difficulties. I was fortunate to meet some awesome experts on a range of topics including ADHD, sensory processing disorder, attachment, and neuropsych evaluations as well as others along the way, many of whom I was fortunate to partner with to provide introductory online education.

Since that time, years passed, and I went back to school to become a Certified Health Coach. I learned about special diets, supplements, stress management, managing sleep issues, positive psychology, etc. A few years after that, I went back to school again and got my master's degree from Maryland University of Integrative Health. I researched and wrote many papers focused on issues facing parents of children with challenges.

Anyway, getting back on task, girlfriends, this book was written just for you! I decided to write this book because I felt there just wasn't enough support for families of children with challenges and I wanted to help with that. I want you to know that you are not alone. Other girlfriends have experienced your struggles and know, like you, that there are many peaks and valleys in raising a child with challenges. You are your child's best advocate, and your heart gives more time, energy and effort than anyone else. My hope is that you will find this book helpful in coming up with ways to manage family stress with your own personal situation. My heart is with you along your journey, and I and many other girlfriends have compassion for what you are going through.

Please enjoy reading this book. I hope you find it helpful.

My best to you,

Robin

HOW THIS BOOK IS ORGANIZED

This book is organized for a quick and simple read. Each chapter has four sections as follows:

Section 1: A brief blurb on a way to address your stress

Section 2: A real-life girlfriend story (or two)

Section 3: Tips you can use based on what I and other girlfriends have learned

Section 4: What I wish I would have known, before I learned it the hard way.

The "girlfriend stories" I share in this book are all based on true stories, but I have changed the names of the girlfriends and their children to protect their privacy.

Finally, please note that this book is for informational purposes only and is not intended to give specific advice on particular medical or mental health issues. You will not be able to diagnose or treat your child from what you learn in this book. Please consult your medical or mental health professional for specific advice on your particular situation.

Robin Bartko

CHAPTER 1

You Are Not Alone

Girlfriends, I decided to write this book because I remember how alone I felt when I realized that my son had challenges. He was my third child and raising him has been completely different than raising my two older children. While my girlfriends with typical children were online shopping for the cutest new outfit and planning their next vacation, I was the parent with many more concerning worries on my mind. My heart hurt as many people really didn't understand the challenges facing families with children who have challenges. I want to assure you that you are not alone. Yes, raising a child with challenges can be very tough, but there are other families that want to support you. Now for a Girlfriend story.

Girlfriend Story:

My girlfriend, Abigail, called up her best friend, Katrina and asked to meet her for coffee. Katrina sensed by the tone of Abigail's voice that something was wrong. When both girlfriends got together for coffee, Abigail confided in Katrina and told her she was having some issues with her daughter. Abigail noticed her daughter behaved very differently than her peers. As good girlfriends do, Katrina listened intently to Abigail, but she really didn't know how to help her. Katrina went home after their coffee meeting and worried about Abigail and her family. Katrina tried to think of who she knew that had a child with challenges and she reached out to her church community. After about a week, someone from her church called Katrina and mentioned she would be happy to talk with Abigail. Katrina's church friend had a long conversation with Abigail, and they shared that they both had a lot of similar parenting challenges. Katrina's church friend became a mentor to Abigail and Abigail didn't feel so alone. Now years later, they are still very good friends.

Girlfriend Tips:

1. Understand that it is OK to feel alone at first

It is only natural to feel alone at first. You are only human. If you are not up to talking with anyone about what you are facing, then write it in a journal. Acknowledging your pain and concern is the first step. Try not to self-medicate to numb the pain you are feeling by eating too much or too little, drinking or using drugs or alcohol. Long term, self-medicating will do more harm than good. Ask yourself, am I self-medicating to numb this pain? Am I having too many glasses of wine? Am I stress eating? Am I smoking to chill my nerves?

2. Reach out to someone you trust when you are ready

When you get the strength to share your struggles, reach out to people who you can confide in. Perhaps it's a girlfriend? A family member? A coworker? Share your worries and ask them to connect you with others who are facing similar challenges. I did this when I was really struggling with my son's challenges. I called one of my best friends, we met, and I had a good cry. It was very emotional, but it helped me acknowledge that I needed help with this situation. Have you ever noticed that sometimes just having a shoulder to cry on is all you need to get more clarity on how to move forward?

3. Connect face-to-face with people confronting similar challenges

Discussing issues online can help, but you can't always feel people's true emotions or intent. I have heard psychologists say this repeatedly, "Nothing substitutes for one on one communication with people." However, if you have no one to reach out to in person then you can start by connecting online and then perhaps by phone, Skype or Zoom. Feel free to email me at Robin@SpecialChildWellness.com if you need assistance in reaching out to other families with children who have challenges or support groups in your area.

* * *

What I Wish I Would Have Known:

I wish I would have known that I am not the only parent raising a child with challenges. I self-medicated a lot to numb my feelings by nighttime eating lots of snack mix and diet soda. I gained a tremendous amount of weight and I really looked and felt terrible. Also, my migraines were more frequent. Being bullheaded, it took me a long time before I acknowledged that my family was struggling and began to reach out for help.

I, also, wish I would have known earlier that not only could my family's stress improve, but also that I could help my child make progress. When we are in a storm, it is often difficult to see beyond it. Have you ever noticed that? Psychologists often use the phrase that the setting was a "perfect storm." To me this means that when things are not going well and are continuing to build up, a storm gets brewing and it is hard to put your life jacket on until it is too late. You don't have to let that be you!

CHAPTER 2

Stress Management 101

We often want our lives to be stress-free and feel like a Hallmark™ movie – especially the Christmas ones! We all hope for a happy ending. However, when raising a child with challenges, perfection is not always possible. Finding peace with our expectations is the key.

Raising a child with challenges is very stressful at times. You should know that how you feel about your stress can really make a difference. Sometimes our emotions get stuck and things are not as bad as we fear. It is important to take a step back and make that determination. If you are stressing about something, you need to ask yourself if what you are fearing is really true. For example, "If my child flunks this test will he really drop out of school?" Or, "Since my child tried vaping, he is going to get into drugs." See how our minds wander to the negative?

Lastly, you have heard the expression, "It takes a village to raise a child." Well, raising a child with challenges takes more than that. It takes some tough skin, understanding, like-minded girlfriends, family and professionals. All these people are there to support you. We girlfriends are there for each other. Don't forget to reach out to others. Reaching out to others can help you get a clear picture of what stresses that you can work on and what stresses that you can learn to accept.

Girlfriend Story:

Years ago, when I had my adoption education and support web site, I organized a conference with several speakers.[1] One of the speakers was Dr. Ronald S. Federici (https://www.drfederici.com), a very well-known and respected neuropsychiatrist in the adoption world with more professional titles than I can list. Dr. Federici is very educated and he isn't just book smart. He has adopted many children himself. He is known for handling some of the most difficult cases in the United States, assisting families with children with challenges such as Fetal Alcohol Syndrome, intellectual disabilities, Autism, Asperger's Syndrome, ADHD, etc.[2]

Anyway, back to the conference. Parents drove in from all over the country to attend the conference. One lady even came from Kentucky to Baltimore! Dr. Federici has a very straight shooter, direct style. He shared his experience of raising his adoptive children and merged it with his expert professional expertise. One word of advice he gave to parents with his evaluation and recommendations for services was that he cannot make everything better for your family, but he probably can help your family's stress improve by 80%. Do not demand perfection because your child is going to have their bad days, but your child can make significant improvement – even some of the children with the most significant challenges. This was great advice that I still carry with me today. Life is not perfect, but the progress we have made with my son from where we started is huge. Dr. Federici knew that all of us needed to hear that there is hope!

Girlfriend Tips:

1. Evaluate your perception of stress

There is a great video by Kelly McGonigal about the perception of stress. It is called "How to Make Stress Your Friend," and it discusses how our perception of stress affects our body and mind. The video discusses a study of over 30,000 people on how they felt about stress and then analyzed the participants death records (I know that sounds kind of morbid, but it really is interesting). It was amazing to learn that how people felt about stress influenced their health. It also discussed the importance of human connection, stress hormones like oxytocin and resilience.[3] Watch it now! Here is the link: https://www.youtube.com/watch?v=RcGyVTAoXEU

How you feel about your stress really matters. If you feel you are doomed, then your body and mind often reflect that. Remember that human connection is very important in managing your stress. Reach out to others, it is not only good for them, but for you as well.

2. Take one step at a time

I remember when I got the diagnosis for my son, I was devastated. I went up to my room and cried my eyes out. I suspected my son had some challenges, but now my fears were confirmed. What was I going to do? After about a week or so I wiped the tears and then went full charge ahead. I had big plans on doing everything I could to help him. I would arrange for this therapy and that therapy and evaluation after evaluation as well as run a household with two other children in it and work at my job. Over the next few months I found myself exhausted. I dragged my son to various therapies and evaluations and was trying to do everything at once.

A friend with a child with challenges then gave me some good advice – slow down and take one step at a time. You only have so much time, energy and financial resources. You are not going to solve or improve my son's challenges overnight and it is not going to be perfect. Just do what you can.

After nearly passing out from exhaustion, I slowed down and took one task at a time. I made notes and made a game plan that was subject to change. Both my son and I were less exhausted and even got some quality time together. Remember that guiding your child is not a sprint, it is a long marathon. Just take the pace that is best for your family.

3. Let go of perfection

This is a really tough one, but it is important! In the above girlfriend story, I discussed what Dr. Federici mentioned about letting go of perfection. When we change our expectations and understand that our children are not always going to fit in a perfect mold, we will find more peace. One of the hardest things with raising my son is that I often felt lonely about his situation and that people really didn't understand. This itself caused me a lot of stress. When I reached out to some of my girlfriends in the adoption community and we would get together, I realized that we were facing some of the same challenges in raising our children. It was a sense of comfort knowing that I was not alone. Reach out to other parents and try to get with them face to face or talk on the phone. Hearing, seeing and feeling other parents' emotions can really help you see stress from a different angle and with a clearer lens. Treat yourself to some self-compassion like you would a good friend so you don't demand so much perfection from yourself.

Girlfriend Story 2:

My husband was brought up very religious and is a God loving man and doesn't like to miss church (although I do sometimes). Every Sunday morning, we get up and go to our local church for services. We prefer to take our children with us. On one Sunday morning, our son was having a particularly bad morning before we left for church. The kiddie cup got thrown on my nice clean outfit, our son was grumpy, and he kicked and screamed the whole time when we were trying to get him dressed. He was really out of sorts that day and the house was extremely loud. I suggested to my husband that he can go on to church with our other kids and I will stay home with our son since he was having a bad morning. My husband didn't want to hear about having my son and I stay home and insisted that the whole family go to church. So, we all went to church and it was a total disaster. Our son yelled and screamed, threw food and little books and we all came home ever more stressed. After emotions calmed down, my husband and I had a "we need to talk" talk.

More Girlfriend Tips:

4. Sit it out sometimes!

I'll say it again, it is ok to sit it out! Sometimes the stress with a child with challenges is off the radar. They may be having a bad day and their symptoms are worse than normal. It is ok to put the brakes on and not attend everything that is planned. Sometimes the stimulation for a birthday party is too much for your child. Perhaps you can cancel going to the party but set up a future playdate for the kids to get together on another day.

In the church girlfriend story above, my husband and I had a good "we need to talk" talk. We decided that, at times, one of us would stay home from church while the other family members attended, or we would each attend church at different times. To be honest, we did get some flak about this, but it was the right choice for our family. Of course, those who haven't raised a child with challenges really don't understand the scope of the stress we endured.

* * *

What I Wish I Would Have Known:

I wish I would have known that there is support in the community for families with children with challenges. It literally took me years to figure this out. For years my heart kept telling me that no one understands what I am going through. I really felt hopeless. Girlfriends, this is simply not true and don't let your mind think of it that way. There is hope! When you realize that others can support you and can relate to what you are going through, your stress will be reduced.

CHAPTER 3

Communicating with Your Child and Significant Other

As a mom to a child with challenges you need to be able to communicate with lots of people. Doctors, therapists, teachers, neighbors, friends, daycare providers and family are just some examples of those you need to engage to take care of your child. For now, let's focus on what I believe is most important – communicating with your child and significant other.

Communicating with your loved ones is not always easy even in the best of circumstances. Sometimes it really can be a challenge, and even more so when dealing with stress. The key is finding how to communicate with someone you love in the way they will perceive it best. A book that I've found very helpful to improve my ability to communicate with loved ones is *The 5 Love Languages* by Gary Chapman. What is presented in the book seems so simple and common sense – everyone has a preference for one or more of five love languages such as "words of affirmation," "acts of service," and "physical touch."[1] It is an excellent book and a quick read, and there are even various versions for teens, military, men, etc. If you have not read it, I highly recommend that you do; it really made a difference for me. You can find it online, in a bookstore or at your local library.

Girlfriend Story:

Years ago, after adopting my son, my husband and I both learned a lesson on the best way to communicate with each other. I was busy running our son around to various therapies, dealing with school issues and managing doctor's appointments. At the end of the day I was exhausted and all I wanted to do was eat something and head to bed. My husband really didn't comprehend why I was tired all the time. He was kind and would sometimes bring me home my favorite treat to eat or some flowers, but I really wasn't that fazed by them. Finally, one day my husband asked me, "What is going on with you?" I responded and said that I hated running all the time and what I really wanted was a someone to take over some of errands and to give me a foot rub. You see, what feeds my soul are "acts of service" from others and "physical touch."

On the other hand, my husband tried to help more, but often frowned in disappointment because I didn't make a big fuss about it. From my perspective, I was like, "It's about time!" I was in no mood for praising him. As time went on, I eventually learned that what feeds his soul is "words of affirmation" – praise. He really liked me showing gratitude to him in a verbal way.

I'm kind of embarrassed to say this, but this really took me years to figure it. Fortunately, now, our communication is much better, and I get many more foot rubs!

Girlfriend Tips:

1. Observe what feeds your loved one's soul

Take time to watch your loved one and try to figure out which way of communicating feeds their soul. Ask them questions such as, "Would you rather have someone help you fold the laundry or buy you a present?" Or, "Would you rather be told that you are doing a great job or get a back massage?" There are great lists of questions in *The 5 Love Languages* series of books.

This holds true for both communicating with your significant other and your child. Just observe them and see what lights them up and feeds their souls.

2. Determine how your loved ones learn best

It is important to try to figure out how your loved one learns best. For years I would constantly give verbal reminders to my son. I would say things like, "Turn the TV down," "Put your shoes on," and "Go to bed now." I would have to tell him multiple times and I often felt ignored by him. Eventually, I realized that he really is a visual learner. I would point to the remote and show him the "volume down" button or I would take his shoe, hand it to him, and point to his feet. He responded much faster.

When I was getting my master's degree I studied various learning styles. What I found fascinating was that when people were required to verbally repeat what they were asked to do, it made the requested action more likely to occur. Also, teaching others what they learned and limiting multitasking helped retention as well.[2] Anyway, you may want to try to ask your child to repeat back what you asked them to do and see what kind of results you get.

3. Use what you've learned!

Once you've figured out the best way to communicate with your loved one, you must really make an effort to do it. Don't get caught up in the "that doesn't work for me" syndrome. The key is what works for your loved one – not what works for you.

4. Forgive yourself if you mess up

It may take a while to figure how best to communicate with your loved ones. People can be complicated and remember it's a long marathon not a sprint. Don't beat yourself up if you mess up. Have patience and keep trying.

* * *

I Wish I Would Have Known:

I wish I would have known more about communication styles years ago. I'm embarrassed to say that I really thought my way was best. I now realize what works for one person does not always work for another. Sometimes just learning about these communication tips helps us see a new perspective.

CHAPTER 4

Fostering a Positive Relationship with Your Child

When you are raising a child with challenges the cold hard truth is that our reality as mom's may not be what we imagined. I know I envisioned snuggling with my kids on a cold morning in bed, reading stories, and making cookies that they loved. I dreamed that my kids were polite, did their chores and that life would be good.

All kids go through developmental milestones, but mom's with children with challenges have much more demands on them emotionally, financially and with time management. The life they dreamed of or envisioned is not the reality of their current situation. Mom's with children with challenges often feel guilt that they don't feel closer to their child and their child doesn't feel closer to them. Also, it is not uncommon that mom's feel upset over other relationships in their life like those with their significant other, other children, and close friends – all of which may have been impacted by the demands of raising a child with challenges.

When I had my adoption education and support website, I worked with Dr. Lark Eshleman https://www.larkeshleman.com/, an awesome professional, to develop a webinar entitled *"Attachment and Adoption: What is it and why is it so important?"*[1] I was blessed to meet Dr. Eshleman several times and even went to her home on one occasion. Dr. Eshleman had experience in dealing with families who had children with post-traumatic stress disorder as well as adoption related issues such as abandonment. She is the author of a great book, entitled *Becoming a Family: Promoting Healthy Attachments with you Adopted Child.* However, you don't have to have an adopted child to have a child with attachment issues. Below are some girlfriend tips I learned from Dr. Eshleman and others regarding attachment, but first let me share a girlfriend story.

Girlfriend Story:

My girlfriend, Amber, adopted a little girl from China. Amber had waited over three long years to bring her child home and she was "beyond the moon" excited. She couldn't wait to play with her little girl, teach her crafts, and dress her up. Amber had read a bunch of parenting books and felt she was ready to be a mom. However, when she arrived home with her little girl, Amber noticed right away that her little girl tended not to look at her. Amber thought to herself, "That's OK, it's just that adjustment time with a new adoption." Months went by and Amber's new little girl still tended to not look her in the eye. Even worse, the little girl freely went to strangers and appeared to give them more affection than she gave to Amber! As a new mom and her daughter's primary caregiver, Amber felt hurt. I saw Amber a few times over the next eight months and she told me everything was going great. However, I could see in her eyes that she had concerns. After celebrating her daughter's second birthday, Amber sent me a text and asked me to meet her at our local pizza shop. I could tell by the tone in Amber's text that she was upset. When we met, she teared up and told me her new little girl hated her and loved everyone else. After some girlfriend hugs Amber pulled herself together and we had a little talk. I asked Amber if she had ever heard about attachment issues. She said, "No." I talked to her about Dr. Eshleman's book, which Amber quickly bought and read. The next time we met she said that she was starting to realize that her child didn't hate her – she was probably having some attachment issues. Amber watched the webinar I developed with Dr. Eshleman and sought help from a professional. That was over five years ago and now you would never know that Amber's child had attachment issues. Amber and her daughter are best buddies!

Below are some girlfriend tips I learned along the way.

Girlfriend Tips:

1. Spend quality time each day with your child

We are all busy with working and raising a family and time flies. It is so easy to get caught up in the details of everyday life and not really spend good quality time with the ones who mean the most to us. Put your cell phone and computer away. Spend quality time with your child doing things he or she likes, whatever it is – building a huge block tower, watching a funny cat video, painting their nails, or playing a fun board game. Tell other family members to not interrupt you unless it is an emergency.

2. Observe your child and look for attachment symptoms

Here are some attachment symptoms from Dr. Eshleman's webinar, *"Attachment and Adoption: What is it and why is it so important?"* to be on the lookout for:

- Is your child looking at you in the eye?
- Does your child go to strangers easily?
- Is your child rigid about routines?
- Does your child squirm around when trying to be held?
- Does your child tend to be inflexible?

3. Try to have way more positive interactions with your child then negative ones

This is often a difficult thing to do with a child with challenges. Your child is running all over the place when the other kids are sitting nicely or your child throws something when other kids are playing calmly. Do you hear yourself telling you child, "Don't touch that? "Don't be so loud?" "You need to try harder?" Girlfriends don't be too hard on yourself. Our brains tend to migrate to the negative. Also, it doesn't help when others keep reminding us of our kids' faults! Although your child's behavior may be driving you and others crazy at times, try to correct them less (unless of course they are putting themselves or someone else in danger). As difficult as it is, find things your child is doing good. One good technique that has worked in our family is when you notice your child doing something good, mention it to someone else in the room in a way your child can hear. For example, I will say to my husband, "Daddy, did you notice that junior put his toys away all by himself?" "Isn't that awesome?" Kids love this!

4. Get help sooner than later

As I mentioned in the "girlfriend story" above, Amber didn't reach out for help for over two years. From my experience I would say that many parents wait even longer than that. If you sense something does not seem typical with your child, make a note in your phone along with the date and your concern. Share your concern with other moms of children with challenges, a support group, a close girlfriend or your pediatrician. Read a book on attachment and look for the symptoms. Seek out a professional. Don't regret not reaching out!

* * *

What I Wish I Would Have Known:

I wish I knew about attachment issues before I became a parent. The typical parenting books discuss developmental milestones but tend not to mention things like attachment. We really need better parenting books that give warning signs, so that parents are more educated on what to look for if their gut is telling them something may not be typical.

Robin Bartko

CHAPTER 5

Building and Rebuilding Relationships

One significant source of stress for moms of children with challenges is the impact it has on our other relationships. This especially includes our significant other, siblings, extended family and close friends. I often hear from girlfriends who are worried about their most important relationships. They sense that their relationships aren't going the way they wanted, but they don't know how to get them back on track. It is a constant worry and frustration on their minds.

Girlfriend Story:

One day when my girlfriend, Lydia, was visiting we watched an old episode of the *Oprah Winfrey Show*. Oprah was interviewing her longtime friend, John Travolta, and his wife, Kelly Preston. John and Kelly were discussing how they were not always on the same page when raising their son, Jett. (Sadly, Jett later passed away from a seizure). Kelly shared that she had to deal a lot with Jett's discipline. John would come home from a movie set and wanted to be their son's playmate – he didn't want to be involved in the discipline. John only wanted positive interaction. This caused friction in the relationship between John and Kelly. When I saw this, I sensed that John and Kelly must have a child with challenges. Years later it became public knowledge that their son, Jett, was on the autism spectrum.

Oprah then asked John and Kelly how they got through this relationship issue and they shared they sought expert advice. They were told to allow Kelly to be the disciplinarian. John could not override her, and he had to always support her in front of their son. This technique worked wonders for them and really helped their relationship. John and Kelly felt supportive of each other and were on the same page with this discipline technique.

After watching this episode of the *Oprah* show, my friend Lydia and I had a very personal discussion about it. We both shared that we struggled at times with our relationships with our significant other and other children. We really appreciated that John and Kelly were so open about their struggles and were able to get past them. It gave both of us hope.

Girlfriend Tips:

1. **Schedule alone time with your significant other and/or your other children**

This was great advice I received years ago that I have truly used. My son with challenges was having tremendous behavior issues. Every time we went out of the house to a restaurant, social event, or other activity we were putting out fires and tension was in the air. My other two children sensed this and when we got home they would just migrate to their bedrooms. These outings were far from "quality time."

I noticed this, felt terrible about it, but didn't know what to do. I was given some excellent advice to schedule weekly one-on-one time with my other children alone. This advice brought awesome results! I felt emotionally more connected with my other children and they did with me. It gave my other children time to confide in me about issues that were bothering them, and it gave us time to have fun together. I would often let my other children pick what they wanted to do (within reason on a girlfriend's budget) like going to local restaurant of their choice or a trip to the local bookstore or library to browse.

2. Reach out for help

One problem girlfriends often have is finding someone to watch their child with challenges. Of course, you can hire someone if you can afford it. If you can't, then reach out to close friends, community groups like your church, your friends, or relatives you trust. Be frank and tell them your situation and ask them if they are interested in helping. Sometimes a widow from church, someone from your extended family, or a compassionate friend can help. Really give looking for someone to help the old "college try." You may need to reach out to ten or more people before you find someone. That is OK and is what happened to me. After many attempts, a friend finally recommended a sitter who had experience with children with challenges. The sitter was awesome, and I felt like I got my family back because it gave me time to strengthen or rebuild relationships. I am so thankful that I did not give up.

3. Schedule one-on-one time at least once per week

It is important that you have a consistent schedule of one-on-one time with those you care about. Don't just think about it, do it! Get it on your schedule. Make a family calendar that you can share on Google with all family members or on a paper calendar in your kitchen, so everyone knows about it. The key is to make it a routine. If an emergency pops up, reschedule it and make up that time. Don't just blow it off until next week! At first, it will be difficult to make this commitment, but your key relationships are well worth making the time.

✳ ✳ ✳

What I Wish I Would Have Known:

Have you ever noticed that it is hard to make good decisions when you are close to a situation? Well, that is what happened to me. I felt terrible about my lack of quality time with my two older children, but I didn't know what to do about it. Since I didn't have anyone in line offering to help me, I also worried about the finances of paying someone. However, when I eventually got assistance for a few hours each week, I realized it was a very small price to pay compared to what really mattered to me. Divorces, broken long term relationships cost a ton both financially and emotionally. Don't make that mistake! It took me a long time to realize that there really are people who want to help. Also, in helping yourself you may also be helping someone else. For example, asking a recent widow to help you may give her a sense of purpose as well.

CHAPTER 6

Dealing with Unsolicited Advice

Dealing with unsolicited advice is a subject that is near and dear to my heart. I have shed many a tear as a result of hurtful comments people have made to me regarding my son's actions or behavior. Just about everyone notices when our child's behavior is not typical. While their reaction to our children's behavior is out of our control, we can reduce our pain by preparing ourselves to deal with it.

We learn a lot about people from what I call their "BS meter," the measure of their annoyance level. How fast someone's "BS meter" reaches its limit comes from a variety of factors including their experiences, personality, genetics and environment. Some people's nature is just easy going and they aren't phased by behavior such as a child jumping up and down on their couch at high speed. Let's call them "high BS meter" people because they can tolerate a lot of BS.

However, this type of behavior drives other people bananas. We'll call them the "low BS meter" people because they can't tolerate hardly any BS. These people are the ones that can make our lives horrible with their unsolicited comments and judgements. As I mentioned before, I developed some thick skin on this subject and have shed many tears when someone made a rude comment to me about my son's behavior. Now for the first girlfriend story.

Girlfriend Story 1:

My girlfriend, Chelsea, is beautiful. She has golden, suntanned skin and wakes up not needing a touch of makeup (I know, I hate that too! It's just not fair). One stroke of the brush and her hair is perfect, not even needing a curling stick or touch up. Anyway, she has an easy going, free spirit personality to go with it. It really takes a lot to get her frazzled. Her son has ADHD and some learning issues and often runs through the house in his underwear and behaves in a way in what some would describe as out of control. When her mother-in-law comes to visit, she constantly tells Chelsea's son to calm down and put on more clothes. In other words, Chelsea's mother-in-law is a "low BS meter" person. Chelsea's mother-in-law requires order and organization.

After a long weekend visit from Chelsea's mother-in-law, even my easy-going Chelsea had enough. Chelsea was upset and called me on the phone while she was running to her room. Her mother-in-law was constantly giving Chelsea unsolicited advice. Sometimes Chelsea's husband would hear the comments, but the reality is that society still seems to have a double standard and we moms tend to get the grunt of it. What Chelsea's mother-in-law didn't understand was that there were many times when Chelsea could not influence her son's behavior. These unsolicited comments made Chelsea feel like a failure. When Chelsea called me, I assured her that she was not a failure and I shared some experiences that my girlfriends and I had with unsolicited advice.

We had a good laugh at these "funny now" stories. Chelsea felt less alone after our discussion.

Girlfriend Tips:

1. Recognize the "low BS meter" people

I can now walk in a room with a group of people and predict which people are the "low BS meter" people. I tell myself, "Be prepared, he or she will probably say something stupid." I prepare myself so that it doesn't emotionally rattle me (well, at least not as much). Now I can even laugh about it. After all, a girlfriend needs to keep her sense of humor to stay sane!

2. Acknowledge that you heard their unsolicited advice

As a way of showing respect, make sure the person making the unsolicited comments knows that you are not ignoring them. For example, Chelsea in our girlfriend story above, may want to say to her mother-in-law, "I'm aware that my son is jumping on the couch and I am not up to discussing this issue right now." This confirms to Chelsea's mother-in-law that she has been heard but lets her know that you don't want to talk about it. It's OK not to confront her in heat of the moment, especially since the individual probably doesn't understand your situation (or might not be in the right frame of mind to learn). Unfortunately, it is not unusual that you may need to repeat your response several times.

3. Seek someone to intercede when the time is right

Have you ever noticed that people are influenced the most by those with whom they are emotionally connected? For example, in our girlfriend story, Chelsea was not comfortable talking with her mother-in-law directly. Instead, she asked her husband to talk with his mom. He was opposed to doing this at first until he sensed through Chelsea's body language how stressed it made her feel. He finally confronted his mom saying, "Did you just ask Chelsea to tell our son to stop jumping on the couch again?" His mom responded, "Yes." Her husband said, "Mom, as I have discussed with you before, you know that our son has some challenges. Have you ever thought about how it makes Chelsea feel when you continuously ask her to stop something that she can't control?"

Keep the conversation short and try to address it when it happens. Asking others to answer questions often makes them think more about the situation. Another possible preventative technique is for Chelsea's husband to have a discussion with his mom <u>prior</u> to her next visit so it is at the top of her mind for awareness. And if Chelsea's husband sees the mother-in-law giving unsolicited advice during her visit, then he should discuss it with her in real time as it happens. Now for one last girlfriend story on this subject.

Girlfriend Story 2:

My girlfriend, Latisha, had a similar situation as Chelsea but with her own mom. Latisha's mom never believed that Latisha's son had challenges and their relationship was getting big-time stressed over it. Have you ever noticed that denial can cause a lot of relationship problems? Anyway, Latisha tried all the above girlfriend tips and they didn't work. She came to me for advice. I must say I gave Latisha an "A" for effort because she really tried to set boundaries with her mom and had no success. The Thanksgiving holiday was coming up in a few weeks and Latisha and her family were planning to go visit her mom and extended family. Latisha always stayed the long weekend with her mom, and it stressed her out. I asked Latisha, "Is there anyone else that she could stay with that lived near her mom?" She indicated that her sister lived only 5 miles from her mom's house. I mentioned that she may want to ask her sister if she could stay with her instead, but to be sure that her mom knew about the change in plans *prior* of her visit. Latisha took my advice and stayed with her sister. She visited her mom for short spurts, but on her terms. She came home much less stressed.

Another Girlfriend Tip:

4. Set your boundaries

Another option if all else fails is to accept that some people just don't get it. If that is the case, spend little or no time with them. They just can't relate. They never raised a child with challenges, and it is not something they can comprehend. These types of people are toxic to your emotionally health! You are in control of your relationships. You don't have to cut them off entirely (unless you want to), but just change the parameters of the relationship. This was a big concept I learned when I was in training to become a health coach and I can tell you that it really works! My health coach instructor had a tough relationship with his dad who favored his brother. He taught us how he kept a relationship with his dad but set boundaries and communication styles by limiting visit durations and setting parameters.

* * *

What I Wish I Would Have Known:

I wish I would have known that others had experienced unsolicited advice and it wasn't just me. I felt alone and got frustrated. It really affected me emotionally. It really upset me. I now know and understand that some people just don't get it and it was a waste of my energy.

CHAPTER 7

Celebrating the Good Stuff and Staying Positive!

Girlfriends, as you know, life can truly be harder for families raising a child with challenges. Our hearts ache for our children and other families who face these challenges. We get plenty of unsolicited advice but too little empathy and support. Caring for our children takes much more time, effort, and finances than we ever imagined (or sometimes even have). We'll do whatever it takes for our child and our family, and in doing so we're often understandably stressed out. Dealing with chronic constant stress can be mega difficult and it can take its toll.

However, there are many times when good things happen in our lives for ourselves and our loved ones. These are the good times that we have longed for! It is important that we take time to celebrate these good times so that we can both enjoy them and remember that good times are possible. As Dr. Rick Hanson, a well-respected psychologist, says, "Your brain is like Velcro for negative experiences and Teflon for positive ones."[1] Isn't that the truth! Our emotions tend to get stuck on remembering the tough times.

You can learn more about this by checking out Dr. Rick Hanson's awesome website at https://www.rickhanson.net/. Now for another girlfriend story.

Girlfriend Story:

Sophia's daughter, Isabella, was really struggling in school. When Isabella brought home her report card she felt ashamed about getting all "C's," "D's," and even some failing grades. Sophia and her daughter were in tears because Isabella had tried so hard. However, Isabella's attention and sensory issues made it difficult for her to stay focused on any topic for very long. One day I suggested to Sophia that she talk to the school psychiatrist about moving her daughter to another classroom with a different teacher. I guess I had put my foot in my mouth because Sophia was offended by what I said. After all, her daughter had friends in that class. Why would Sophia want to disrupt that? I regretted making the suggestion and didn't bring it up again. However, I knew through the girlfriend network that her daughter's teacher was very inexperienced and not the best fit for a child with Isabella's challenges.

Some time went by and Sophia got an update on her daughter's grades. Her daughter's grades were even worse. Sophia was understandably upset and emailed the school psychiatrist to ask for a meeting. The school psychiatrist discussed Sophia's concerns about her daughter and asked if she would be willing to have Isabella move to another class with a teacher that better fit her learning style. Sophia said she would consider it and had a discussion with her daughter that night. Isabella said she would give it a try. The new teacher, who had over 30 years of experience, lit up when she saw Isabella and asked her lots of questions. "What helps you learn best?" "What do you like to learn about?" Sophia's daughter settled into her new class and later was asked to write a paper on her favorite animal. She chose to write about the koala bear. The grade came back and much to Sophia and her daughter's surprise, she received her first "A."

Sophia called me to tell me what happened and thanked me. I got tears in my eyes because I was so happy. I mentioned to Sophia to tell everyone she knew about her daughter's great "A." She and her daughter told her grandparents, family, friends and coworkers. She indeed celebrated the good stuff! Both Sophia and her daughter felt more hope and her grades continued to improve.

Girlfriend Tips:

1. Look for the positives

It can sometimes seem hard to find things that a child with behavioral, emotional and/or learning challenges is doing well. Look for anything you can find positive about your child and talk to them about it for at least 20-30 seconds. Don't be afraid to get animated and add a "high five" or "happy dance." Do whatever makes your child know that you are pleased. Another technique that is sometimes even more effective is to have your child overhear you telling someone else how happy or proud you are about what they have done. Never forget that our children want to please us (well, at least sometimes) – even through the hormone driven emotional teen years.

2. Reward the behavior

Some kids respond to rewards and others respond to a reduction in punishment. You know your child best, so you determine what will work for them. In our above girlfriend story, after Sophia makes a big fuss about her daughter's "A," she can offer a reward such as taking her to the zoo if she gets another "A'" or "B" in the next couple of weeks. In her case, it is great to get the teacher on board with this too.

Another option is to reduce an existing punishment. For example, your child doing something well may get a reduction of video game restrictions for a day. Also, as you consider rewards, realize that some kids (and adults) thrive on experiences while others thrive on receiving gifts. Observe and ask your child what they love. Some kids may love to get a video game gift card or a pack of sports cards. Other children may love to get their nails done, go on a little shopping spree, or receive a new outfit. The key is finding whatever feeds your child's soul.

3. Limit your whining

This is some good advice that I received from an expert several years ago that is easier said than done but is really important. It's not that you cannot whine, but that you should limit your whining. The expert told me to tell a good friend or loved one what I was worried about and really let loose and don't hold back my emotions. (Let's face it, a girl needs to vent sometimes!) I took this advice and I had a very bad cry on one of my best girlfriend's shoulders. However, once you share your concerns, don't continuously repeat them because it just brings you back to those upsetting emotions. Let it go! Ouch, I know that this is tough to do but it really is important. If you want to learn more about why whining is bad for your health just look at the brain scans of chronic complainers![1] Constantly complaining really isn't good for our health. That is why it is better to spend more of your time looking for positive interactions versus negatives ones.

4. Be an optimist – it's contagious

Have you ever gotten home and everyone in the family is in a bad mood? We all tend to follow suit and get in a bad mood too. Well, when we celebrate the good stuff, we lift the mood up. Susie, my girlfriend who I worked with for many years, is a ray of sunshine. Whenever Susie showed up with her easy-going smile I knew our office staff would laugh and everyone would be in a better mood. Hanging around people who are optimistic can really set the tone for seeing the world in a more positive light and being more appreciative. Try to spend time with these kinds of people to inspire yourself to be that kind of person!

Something to Ponder ...

Have you ever seen the movie, *Pretty Women*? (I just love Romcom movies!) Well, there is a scene in that movie where Julia Roberts says to Richard Gere, "The bad stuff is easier to believe, you ever notice that?"[2] It is so true! Sometimes when life is not going well, our minds get stuck on the problems, not the solutions.

The thing is that our brains tend to be wired toward the negative. Our emotions take over and we remember and hold on to the hurt and frustration. I think the scientific term is "negativity bias." When we let our emotions hold on to a good thing that has happened – even for just 20-30 seconds – it registers in our brain and sticks with us more.[3]

* * *

What I Wish I Would Have Known:

I wish I would have known that others did not perceive my child's behavior as bad as I thought. I really felt like my child was the worse in the class and all the other kids were model students. I wish I was more focused on what my son did right and let more of the other stuff go. Also, I wish I would have not fretted and complained so much and that I had more positive interactions with my child. Now that I know about his challenges, I am more accepting. However, girlfriends, do not beat yourself up on the past. We are all only human.

CHAPTER 8

The Medication Decision

A very difficult decision for moms of children with challenges is whether or not to medicate their child. Many girlfriends have told me how difficult and stressful this decision was for them. I know, as I was one of those who waited years before even considering medication for my son. As a health coach, my inclination is to look for natural remedies to the greatest extent possible, so this was a big decision for me and my family as well. I worried about what the potential long-term effects might be on my child. When a girlfriend comes to me about their struggles with this issue, I always tell them it is very important for them to think about and research their options.   You must do what you believe is best for your child and your family.

Girlfriend Story:

My girlfriend, Jada, and I took our boys to a local Chick-Fil-A® for some lunch. I was looking forward to some mom-to-mom conversation and for our boys to play together. My son, who was about four or five years old at the time, rushed through eating his meal and then flew into the playground area. I didn't mind because my son needed to burn off some excess energy. Jada's son followed suit and ran into the playground area as well, where three or four other kids around the same age were already patiently waiting to go down the slide.

My very excited son couldn't wait to get on the slide, so he pushed himself to the front of the line. Just then the mom of a typical child – a beautiful little girl who was dressed to a T (let's call her "little angel") – gave me "the look." I went to my son and reminded him that butting in line was not appropriate. My son then went to the climbing part of the playground area and butted in line there, too. This time, "little angel's" mom took matters into her own hands and told my son not to butt in line, followed by giving me a look that clearly communicated, "What's wrong with you, can't you control your kid?"

By this time, my nerves were starting to get a little frazzled. When my son then accidently bumped "little angel," her mom started yelling at me at the top of her lungs. This time she actually said, "Why can't you control your kid?" "Your kid is a bully!" I got so flustered from being yelled at in front of everyone in the restaurant that I took hold of my son's hand and flew out of there.

After I calmed down and found my zen (as much as I could), I took some time to reflect. Sadly, this was just one of numerous similar situations. It was clear that my son's behavior was causing stress both in public and at home. This wasn't good for him or our family. That's when I started considering having my son evaluated for medication.

Girlfriend Tips:

When deciding whether to get an evaluation for medication for your child, consider the following:

1. Determine if your child's behavior is causing profound family stress

Are you, your significant other, or your other children constantly concerned about your child's behavior? When you go somewhere is your child running around crazy and not sitting down nicely like the other kids? Is your child the loudest child in a group? Does he/she freak out when they hear a loud noise? Is your head going back and forth because you need to watch your child more closely than other parents of children of the same age? Are you afraid your child may hurt himself or another person? Are other parents and family members pointing out your child's non-typical behaviors? Does your child constantly rush through things including brushing (or not brushing) their teeth, homework and chores? Is your child constantly disorganized and can't find their shoes, homework assignments, etc.? Girlfriends, really take time and think about your responses to the above questions. There's no magic formula about how many "yes" answers result in profound family stress. However, girlfriends, I am confident that you'll know.

2. Document your child's behavior

If you decide that your child's behavior is causing profound family stress, then take a day or two to document his/her behaviors. A weekend day is usually best because we tend to be with our children the most on these days. Take a paper and pen (or use your phone) and jot down the unusual behaviors you observe and how you, your family, friends and even strangers are responding to them. Remember to keep in mind the age and development of your child. For example, a two-year-old is going to have different behaviors than a ten-year-old.

3. Stop making excuses for your child's behavior

Have you gone to a family gathering and tried to explain your child's behavior by telling everyone that your child didn't sleep well last night? Or, are you apologizing at your place of worship because your child is loud and out of control? At a birthday party, is your child running around like they are on sugar high when the other kids are sitting at the table singing happy birthday?

Girlfriends, how did you answer the above questions? Are you finding yourself making excuses for your child's behavior? If that is the case, then your child's behavior is causing your family significant stress. Stop making excuses. Consider getting your child an evaluation.

4. Follow your gut

You spend the most time, energy, money and worry with regards to your child. You know your child best. Do you feel the stress is taking a toll on your child, yourself, your significant other and other children? Follow your gut. Sometimes having a discussion with a good girlfriend about this subject can help bring clarity to your mind. Remember that getting an evaluation regarding medication is just gathering information. You can decide once you have all your facts.

5. Make a decision for an evaluation

If your list is long and you find yourself constantly making excuses for your child, it's time to make a decision. You know your child best. Do you feel that the stress is taking a toll on your family? Be honest with yourself. In the end, trust yourself and make a decision. Don't ignore the issue.

As you consider your decision, know that getting a medication evaluation is just gathering information. You can decide once you have all your facts. The pediatrician can look at your list, evaluate your child, and make a recommendation or refer you to another professional (such as a psychiatrist) as appropriate. It also may be helpful to know that any decision to use medication is not a "forever" decision. Medication may be right for this phase of your child's development. Please know that you can (and should) reevaluate the use of medication periodically.

Finally, you and your medical professional may decide that medication is not the right answer. There are natural supplements, essential oils, special diets, therapies, etc. that can be helpful and may be used. There are choices. However, never make these decisions alone. You need to be very careful giving supplements and medications because using them incorrectly can have serious consequences. The key is to know your options, work with a medical and mental health professional, and make the decision that is right for your child and your family.

* * *

What I Wish I Would have Known:

Personally, I wish I would have gotten my son evaluated sooner. I really waited too long. I think most parents that I've talked with wait too long as well. Remember, it is just an evaluation. Make the choice that is best for your child and family once you have the facts.

CHAPTER 9

Managing School Issues

Many children with challenges struggle in school because of emotional, learning and/or behavior problems in class. As a result, our children may get into more trouble with peers, teachers and administrators. Not fully understanding the situation, teachers can turn to us in frustration thinking that we can fix the problem by having a heart-to-heart conversation with our child. Unfortunately, this rarely works as we often struggle to get our children to comply as well!

Getting homework completed can also raise the household stress level off the charts. Homework is often rushed through, incomplete, or takes longer to finish than with a typical child. In addition, adding procrastination to the mix, makes it harder to get the homework even started which can result in even more stress.

Girlfriend Story:

My girlfriend, Camila, had a son in middle school when she gave me a call. Her son's puberty was already in full swing. Her son had ADHD and mood issues as well which caused him to get in a lot of trouble with his teachers. He already had a 504 Plan[1] but was really struggling both behaviorally and academically.

Camila was upset and frustrated. Her son's teachers kept calling her at work to tell her about her son's latest behavior and academic issues. One day she received seven separate calls! Camila's boss started to notice all the calls and was getting frustrated with the interruptions. Her boss was concerned it was keeping Camila from getting her work done.

I asked Camila, "Have you tried to establish a different communication arrangement with your son's teachers?" She paused and asked what I meant. I said, "When I had the problem of teachers contacting me at work, I asked that they only contact me via email unless it was an absolute emergency." Camila paused and told me she had no idea that was even an option.

I heard from Camila about two weeks later after she had notified all her son's teachers that she preferred email communication. She said that her stress level at work went down tremendously after only two days. She gave me the biggest hug the next time I saw her! Camila also learned that she could use the emails as documentation for additional educational services for her son, if needed.

Girlfriend Tips:

1. **Set boundaries**

The above girlfriend story demonstrates that changing the communication preference to email only allowed Camila to respond to teacher emails when it was convenient for her. Camila set a boundary with the teachers that really helped her reduce her stress level while she was at work.

2. Get the school psychologist and/or guidance counselor involved

If you are really struggling with your child's behavior and/or academics, email the school psychologist or guidance counselor and arrange a time to talk with them on the phone. I have found that if you give them details of the problem then they can become a valuable liaison between you, your child, and the teacher. My girlfriend, Kathy, had a teacher that was not a big fan of her son. She found that reaching out to the school psychologist really helped the situation from getting worse. A school psychologist and guidance counselor can also serve as someone your child can talk to when they are frustrated or upset.

3. Ask for help with homework

In my experience, if a child is really struggling with their homework, it is very difficult for a mom (or any parent) to help them through it. I've found that it can really increase the stress on your relationship with your child. A tutor, a teacher willing to work with your child after hours, a specialized ADHD (or other) coach, or a gifted peer may be a better answer. Help can be provided in-person or online (e.g., FaceTime or Skype). There are many more resources than there used to be. Reach out to the guidance counselor, school psychologist, or your local parent support group, all of which usually have a list of resources.

* * *

What I Wish I Would have Known:

I wish I would have comprehended at that time that educators are human too and often are contacting us because they are frustrated — just like we are sometimes as moms. I also wish I knew that you do not have to be afraid to ask for your child to be put into a class with another teacher if he/she is really struggling. Sometimes a more experienced teacher — or a teacher with a different teaching style or personality — is just what is needed. Finally, I wish I would have known that the huge homework battles would get better. With guidance, your child will mature and eventually take on more responsibility and become more self-sufficient.

CHAPTER 10

Respite Care

Respite care is when someone temporarily takes care of your child so that you get a break from the daily stress. Let's face it, raising a child with challenges is often tough. With the demands of parenting, our relationships and work, we often forget or have no energy to take care of ourselves. With more health, behavior, and school concerns, raising a child with challenges takes much more time, energy, and financial resources than a typical child. Girlfriends, cut yourself a break! You need it and it is OK to take some time for yourself! Our brains and bodies need respite. And, after all, it's a marathon not a sprint. Your child and family need you for the long run – don't burn yourself out.

Girlfriend Story:

Years ago, when my family was really struggling with stress, we reached out to a professional who asked us, "Why aren't you getting any help?" My first excuse was that I had no one to help. It was a legitimate excuse. My mom had passed away years before and I had three children to worry about. I really didn't have anyone standing in-line offering to help. The professional then asked,

"Have you reached out to your community of family, friends, church, coworkers, etc.?" My response was, "No." However, the question did make me think. I said to myself, "No one really wants to consistently help, so why ask?"

It didn't take long for the stress to get out of hand again, so I decided to reconsider. I called a few friends and received several recommendations for sitters who had experience caring for children with challenges. I ended up getting someone who was highly recommended for several hours each week. At first I was concerned about the finances, but then I realized it was a lot cheaper than if my marriage failed or my relationships with my other children and friends collapsed. This gave me a chance to spend time with my older children and husband, as well as to just take some time to relax. ***This was some of the best advice I ever got.***

After about six weeks of having a sitter I noticed that I had dropped a little weight that I was trying to lose, and I got less frustrated with my children. My older kids confided in me more, and they knew that there was one-on-one time during which they could reach out to me when necessary. Lastly, I felt hope. Respite care helps rebuild relationships that were important to you.

Girlfriend Tips:

1. Plan for your respite care

You must plan for your own respite care. Don't wait for someone else to volunteer or arrange it for you. I don't want to hear "shoulda, coulda, woulda." Get your respite care time on your calendar. Record it in your phone, weekly planner and set reminders. Do it as often as you can. At least once a week is great.

Worried about finances? There are some organizations that will provide it for you free of charge. Feel free to email me for more information.

2. Do something you love

Perhaps you love to get a massage, to read a good book uninterrupted, to take a walk, to cook a special meal, to go to a movie with a girlfriend, watch sports or do a craft. Perhaps you feel guilty about not spending enough time with your significant other or your other children. Start making a list in your phone now of the things you would love to do and who you want to do them with.

3. Avoid whining while relaxing

On respite? Don't spend your time whining! Sorry for the bluntness, but it's the truth! When you take time for respite, take time to do something that recharges your soul – not something that makes you down, upset or frustrated like going over your problems or challenges. Relax and enjoy, you deserve it!

4. Make respite care a priority

Have you ever made a new year's resolution that you kept for a couple of weeks and then quit? Well, that's what sometimes happens with respite care. Everyone starts with good intentions, but when the sitter is late, money is tight, they have no energy left to plan or life gets busy then they push it off. Don't use these things as an excuse. Make respite care a priority! Girlfriends you need it.

* * *

What I Wish I Would Have Known:

I wish I had realized this really important fact – taking breaks are essential for your health and your relationships. Unfortunately, I really didn't even consider respite care until the professional recommended it. My family and I really needed respite care way before we started it; I really regret not getting respite care sooner. I have noticed that many other families put off getting respite care as well. Girlfriends, respite care is one of the most important things you can do for your family. Make it a priority!

CHAPTER 11

Parent Training & Support

When I was getting my master's degree, my assignments required me to conduct a lot of research and write many papers. One assignment was to identify what research shows to be most effective in reducing stress in parents of children with challenges. This assignment really made me think as I had no idea what the answer would be. Diet, therapies, supplements, medication and more all crossed my mind. After extensive research I was surprised by what I found – *parent training was one of the top ways to reduce parental stress.* [1]

Parental training? You heard right! Training on a wide variety of topics including how best to respond to your child, keeping good relationships with siblings, staying on the same page with your partner, and reducing marital stress can really make a difference. I have taken multiple courses developed for parents of children with challenges from organizations such as *The Arc* and *CHADD*, both in-person and online. Thanks to the Internet this training is more accessible, affordable, and convenient than ever before. However, I strongly recommend live training when available. Be careful, like everything else, not all parental trainings are well done. I remember taking one parent training class and it was absolutely terrible and a waste of my time and money. However, in one of the first trainings I took, the instructor told me that I had so much experience I should be teaching the class. Use your girlfriend network for references, look for reviews or email me at Robin@SpecialChildWellness.com for some resources available.

Parent support groups are important, too. Besides being a place to learn from and share with others, they are also a great resource for finding professionals including physicians, psychiatrists, psychologists, and therapists (such as cognitive behavior, dialectical behavior therapy (DBT), developmental vision, ABA, sensory integration, speech pathologist and occupational therapists). You can learn a lot from other parents about these professionals including the insurance they take, how they interact with children, the politeness of their staff, and the scheduling process – great information that will help you find the best fit for your child.

Girlfriend Story:

My girlfriend, Cindy, took an in-person parent training at a local chapter of *The Arc* along with her husband. He thought it was a stupid idea and was only there because she nagged him to do so. While the parents in this small group of about eight people had children with various challenges, what they all had in common was that their lives were difficult. When some parents expressed how they felt about situations that occurred when raising their child, others shared how they dealt with similar situations. Also, they shared if they regretted their responses and how they wished they would had dealt with it.

Cindy's husband listened intently to the other attendees. After the training was completed, I ran into Cindy at a local mall and asked her how it went. She said, "I can't believe it! My husband thanked me for nagging him to take that class. He has been more considerate to my feelings when I am struggling with our son and he doesn't see me as a nag anymore. This course helped renew my faith in my marriage and our communication has improved." This was wonderful news to hear from Cindy, and I was happy that she was more at peace.

Girlfriend Tips:

1. Make parent training a priority

Girlfriends, I know that you are short on time and probably are low on energy, but it really is important that you put parent training at the top of your list. Raising a child with challenges takes special training. Don't feel bad that you are not an expert at it or that it does not come naturally to you. Take time to learn from others that have dealt with similar challenges. Believe me, parenting my third child who has ADHD has been in a whole different ballpark than raising my first two children. Parent training is worth putting your time and effort into.

2. Take parent training that is taught by those who really know what it is like raising a child with challenges

Girlfriends, it is really important to choose a really good parent training course. I have found that the best courses are taught by those who have raised a child with challenges or have been very involved with children with challenges. I have taken multiple types of these trainings and some of them were a waste of my time.

Robin Bartko

Check with other girlfriends in your area and ask them for some feedback on which parent training is best. Feel free to email me if you haven't found a good course in your area or online for some resources. I think the *in-person* parent training courses are best, but interactive online classes are the next best thing and are convenient.

3. Use what you learned

Once you decide on the parent training and support, be sure you interact with others in the group. Some of the best learning I have seen is when parents ask questions to other parents and professionals. When we interact with others in this way, the light bulb often goes off in our head on how to interact with our own child. You know what I mean, like the aha moment Oprah talks about. Once you have learned techniques that apply to your own situation, start using them! This is where many girlfriends fall short. They take the classes and training, but never use the stuff. You can do all the training, but if you never convert it to your own life with your child, then it is a waste of your time. Don't let that be you!

Some Other Things to Ponder ...

Sadly, from my experience, the stress of raising a child with challenges takes its toll and many parents of children with challenges split up. These broken relationships often cause even more stress, especially for women, both emotionally and financially. Put on your happy face and work hard to save your relationships that are important to you. Parent training can help improve your relationships.

Also, from my experience, girlfriends will share more intimate details with each other if we are talking to each other on the phone or in person. Here is an example, I was thinking of trying a new therapist for my son. I asked my friend, Rosa about a particular therapist because I knew she had used him before for her daughter. Rosa and I played some phone tag, but finally caught up with each other. Rosa mentioned that this therapist was very good, but his office staff was extremely rude and if you need to schedule an appointment then do it right away and don't you dare reschedule the appointment because the office staff isn't good about changing appointment dates. I thought about this and decided I could live with the scheduling issues if the therapist is really good. I tried the therapist for my son and months later my son got the flu and I had to cancel his appointment and try to reschedule it. The cancelling went well, but the rescheduling was really a pain in the butt. Rosa told me so, I was prepared for this. I was willing to put up with the office staff issues because the therapist was excellent.

Another thing to ponder is that sometimes, girlfriends are venting their frustrations and are feeling stressed and the online discussions can get negative, nasty and not productive. Be aware of this. When communicating online, you can't hear people's tone of voice or emotions, so it is not always reflective of what they truly meant. Be careful you don't get caught up in this negativity trap.

* * *

What I Wish I Would Have Known:

I wish I would have taken parent training much earlier than I did. I had no idea it even existed. Years and years went by before I took parent training. It really was worthwhile for my mental health and relationships especially with my other children and spouse. Also, once I took the parent trainings, not only did I feel less alone, I had more confidence in my ability to help my son.

CHAPTER 12

Finances

Worry about finances can really set the stress-o-meter off the radar for many girlfriends – especially girlfriends who have children with challenges. Let's face it, a child with challenges often costs more to raise given the additional costs for medication, doctor's appointments, education supplementation, and various therapies. Girlfriends, I've been there and feel your pain on this subject. Now for another girlfriend story.

Girlfriend Story:

My girlfriend, Raven, is a single mom and even though she works her tail off at work, she struggles financially. After rent, insurance, child care and food, there are very few resources left. Raven has two children. Her youngest son has high functioning autism and ADHD. Raven's son was often perceived by others as rather awkward and didn't communicate well with his peers, teachers and adults. Raven really wanted her son to take an intense social skills course, but she did not have the funding to do it. Raven sent me a text and mentioned she wanted to talk. We got together, and Raven told me her concern. I told Raven that I thought that she had two options. The first is that I was confident that we could find her some funding, but it may take a while to get it. The second was that she could take a course herself and then work with her son daily. Raven thought about what I mentioned and decided to take a course and work with her son daily. I had mentioned this to Raven because I not only knew other parents who had success with this approach, but I also read a book years ago by a therapist that said you really can help your child by working with them for one hour a day. That hour must be focused on your child directly and all other distractions like cell phones, TVs, computers, etc. must be put away. Raven took my advice and attended a course on how to teach her son social skills.

At first, Raven, was exhausted and felt she wasn't making any progress with her son. After all, Raven really was juggling trying to find the time and energy to help her son every day. However, one day Raven took both her sons to a large extended family picnic and she got to observe her youngest son firsthand. An older Aunt came up to her son and asked what was new with him? Her son responded appropriately saying he was busy with school and had a short discussion, and he even had some eye contact with the Aunt. Raven was thrilled! She had worked with her son on improving his eye contact and responses. Previously, Raven's son was perceived as being rude, especially when he didn't make eye contact. It was the first time Raven was able to see her son's social skills improving. Raven was so happy that her effort to help her son was making a difference.

Girlfriend Tips:

1. Look for help with funding

There is funding available for families with children with challenges if you really look for it. You can start with your local chapter of *The Arc*. Often, people think *The Arc* only supports lower functioning children, but that is not true.[1] You can also call your local social services office and ask them for a list. Additionally, there are various nonprofits that may be able to provide some funding as well. The paperwork is often a real pain and sometimes there are income restrictions, but you really can get funding. I have also had girlfriends get funding assistance from their place of worship. One caring fellow parishioner even let my girlfriend use their vacation home for a week for some respite time. If you can't locate funding in your hometown area, then email me at Robin@SpecialChildWellness.com and I will see what I can help you find in your local area.

2. Consider online options to save money

With the Internet there are more online services (classes, instruction, therapies) than ever before. Although in-person services are highly recommended, online may be the next best option if you can't afford in-person services. Many of these online services are either available on-demand or you can schedule a virtual appointment. The quality of these trainings varies. Feel free to email me for available services that I believe are worthwhile.

* * *

What I Wish I Would Have Known:

I wish I would have known about the various funding options when my son was younger. Finances can be a tough subject, especially when you are paying for child care, housing, food, and more already. Getting a child services at an early age is really critical to their success. Don't wait until it is so late that your child can't make progress, or until your child is at the age when you can no longer directly influence their care. I have seen that many girlfriends wait way too long to get help for their child even though they sensed their child was struggling for many years. This situation is especially common when a child gets their first real job or goes off to college and they come home because things are not working out. That is often the time when the "red light" comes on for girlfriends, who then wished they had gotten more help for their child when they were younger.

CHAPTER 13

Self-Compassion

What is "self-compassion?" My definition is "to be constructively not so hard on yourself." Basically, to acknowledge we are human and to cut ourselves a break. Do you ever say things to yourself like: "I really screwed this up," "I am a terrible mom," "Parenting isn't supposed to be this hard, what am I doing wrong?" or "Will I ever get through this tough time in my life?" If so, you may need to practice more self-compassion.

We are often not as warm or kind to ourselves as we are to others. Do we sometimes park or ignore our problems because we just don't feel like dealing with them? That is where self-compassion comes in. We learn how to acknowledge our problems and learn how to find balance with our emotions through the ups and downs of life so we can process them more appropriately.

When I started health coaching, one thing that really surprised me was that people are harder on themselves than I expected. We tend to cut a friend a break more than ourselves. Our emotions get tied up and we often don't really forgive ourselves by chalking up our faults to having a bad day or for only being human. That is where self-compassion comes into play. We need to learn to observe our own behaviors, be less judgmental of ourselves, and cut ourselves a break more.

The guru of self-compassion is Kristin Neff, Ph.D. She has researched this topic in depth and has applied it to her own life. She is the mother of a boy with autism, so she understands the challenges that many families of children with challenges face. She "gets it," meaning she really understands the challenges our families face. In her book, *Self-Compassion*, she discusses these challenges and is not afraid to touch on difficult topics such as parenting, relationships, and sex – all of which have been impacted in her own life story.[1] She also has some good videos that you can check out online.

Girlfriend Story:

My girlfriend, Tai, was facing many challenges. Her relationship with her husband was not going well, her son was having many behavioral and minor medical issues, and she was worried about her finances. Tai called up her best friend, Cassandra, and asked her to come over as she finally had the courage to share what she had been struggling with. Cassandra came over to Tai's house and they sat on the couch. Tai's eyes were puffy, and her mascara was running down her face. Cassandra could sense the distress Tai was having, gave her a hug, and asked her what was wrong. Tai and Cassandra sat on the couch and had a two-hour-long girlfriend conversation. Cassandra had no idea that Tai was struggling with so many issues. Cassandra listened intently without judgement. After Cassandra went home, Tai felt comforted that she had shared her challenges with Cassandra.

A few days later, Cassandra texted Tai to check on her. She told her that it was understandable to be upset when so many challenges were coming to the surface at once and that she shouldn't be so hard on herself. Cassandra helped Tai acknowledge her problems and see them from a compassionate perspective. Cassandra wanted to help out so she insisted on watching Tai's son once a week, so Tai could run errands with less stress. Now that's girlfriend support at its best!

Some time went by and Tai realized she needed even more support in her life. She eventually hired a permanent babysitter to watch her son once a week. Having the permanent sitter improved her relationship with her husband and gave her time to recharge so that she felt she was able to roll with life's ups and downs better. She even arranged to have a family member watch her son when the babysitter was not available. Both Tai's perception of and actual stress reduced enormously.

Girlfriend Tips:

1. Get the book, *Self-Compassion*, by Kristin Neff, Ph.D.

You can check for it at your local library or get it online. This is a great book to learn more about self-compassion. It really goes into detail about ways you can have more self- compassion for yourself.

2. Practice self-compassion exercises

Go to Kristin Neff's web site, https://self-compassion.org/category/exercises/, and try some of the *"Self-Compassion Guided*

Meditations and Exercises."[2] These exercises are quick and insightful.

3. Take a workshop on self-compassion

If you are a more "hands on" kind of girlfriend, then you might want to consider taking a self-compassion workshop. Check them out using the following link: http://self-compassion.org/events/category/short-workshops/

4. Talk with your girlfriends about how you really feel and get their perspective

Arrange a time and talk with a girlfriend either in person or on the phone and open up your heart. Tell them how you really feel about what you are struggling with. Many girlfriends are compassionate and care like no other. This will help you gain more perspective on what you are dealing with.

* * *

What I Wish I Would Have Known:

I wish I would have learned about self-compassion many years ago. I had never even heard of it. I reflect back now and see that I was sometimes my worst critic and that I had some unreasonable expectations of myself. Also, from my experience, many of my girlfriends were extremely hard on themselves as well. Don't waste time, girlfriends! Learn more about self-compassion. You deserve it!

CHAPTER 14

Meditation

I really didn't know much about meditation until I had to take a class on it. The class required a lot of interaction between students, with each of us having to role-play as both a meditation coach and the coach's student. My first thoughts about meditation were, "I don't have time for this," and "Does it really work?" I guess I envisioned a Buddha-like character sitting on a cushion for hours at a time. Well, that was incorrect (however, you can use a cushion if you want to). Meditation practices can be as short as five or ten-minute intervals, and they can be focused on various topics. My favorite is a meditation that involves gratitude.

As my semester on meditation came to an end, I began to become a believer in meditation. I felt my classmates and I had really made progress. We had to rate ourselves on things such as how judgmental we were of others, flexibility, attention span, self-awareness, and labeling our thoughts. We performed this evaluation both at the beginning and end of the semester. My partner and I both rated ourselves as being more flexible and less judgmental after that semester's meditation instruction. However, what really won me over to meditation was when I saw the difference in brain scans (EEG, fMRI, PET, or SPECT scans) of people who did and did not practice meditation. Girlfriends, go to "University of Google" and check them out. It is amazing!

Girlfriend Story:

When I was taking my meditation course during my master's degree program, I heard about a school in Baltimore (not too far from where I live) that was giving meditation a try. The school was in a very underprivileged neighborhood where many of the kids are struggling for food, worrying that their electricity would be cut off, and concerned for their safety. Homelessness was also not uncommon.

The school tried something different – replacing detention with meditation. The instructors admitted that the kids that came to them were often tough kids that were wound up, angry and frustrated. The instructors would teach the kids meditation and how to self-regulate, often using deep breathing techniques. The results were amazing! Many of the kids that were labeled "troubled" were getting in trouble less. There was more peace in the school and the teachers were spending more time teaching instead dealing with behavior issues.[1] See for yourself by watching a short video from CNN:
https://www.cnn.com/2016/11/04/health/meditation-in-schools-baltimore/index.html

There are several nonprofits that are sponsoring meditation in schools. One in the Baltimore area is the Holistic Life Foundation (https://hlfinc.org/). Another organization is the Hawn Foundation (https://mindup.org/thehawnfoundation/), established by actress Goldie Hawn (aka Private Benjamin, actress from the *First Wives*

Club, partner of Kurt Russell and mom to actress, Kate Hudson), which produced the MindUP™ program.[2] Come on, have you ever seen Goldie Hawn when she was not chilled out or when she didn't have a big smile on her face? This meditation stuff must be working!

Girlfriend Tips:

1. Give it a try!

Meditation may not be for everyone, but it really is helping many. Both children and adults can benefit from various forms of meditation. Many integrative services like meditation are even being used in Veterans Administration clinics throughout the United States for those with PTSD and other ailments.[3] Give it a try! It doesn't cost you a fortune and can be done quickly.

2. Start with five or ten minutes

You don't need a lot of time to do meditation. Try it for five or ten minutes first thing in the morning or in the evening just before bed. You can build up more time as your progress with it. The key is doing it daily. Set your cell phone timer to remind yourself that it is time to meditate.

3. Visit the "Your Skillful Means" website

Not sure how to meditate? Check out the meditation practices on the "Your Skillful Means" (http://yourskillfulmeans.com) website. This website is awesome and literally has hundreds of types of meditations to try. At the top, go to "Practices" and select "Psychological, Spiritual or Others."[4] My girlfriends' list of favorites is the "Angel," "Gratitude," "Mountain," and "Walking" meditations. There are other more psychological based meditations that are for activating your parasympathetic nervous system (to chill you out) and for reducing anxiety.

4. Commit to at least six weeks

You may not see immediate results, so develop a plan and commit to following it for at least six weeks. We often jump out of bed and start the day running, so be proactive and schedule your meditation in your day. If you keep at it, I believe you will see that meditation can not only really make a difference in how you respond to people, but also positively impact your relationships with those who are most important to you.

5. Take a meditation class

Many people find it helpful taking a class on meditation. They can learn from the instructor and other students and often make new friends, too. To find a local meditation class near you, just google "meditation class" and your zip code and check out your local resources. Many yoga centers also have meditation classes.

* * *

What I Wish I Would Have Known:

Honestly, I wish I would have started practicing meditation earlier in my life especially after adopting my son when the stress-o-meter was off the radar. It is also helpful when you experience an untimely death or divorce in your family, as well as if you are dealing with relationship issues, medical challenges, or job transitions. I have found that some girlfriends also find it helpful for dealing with chronic back pain, migraines, and digestive issues.

Robin Bartko

CHAPTER 15

Yoga

Yoga is a great exercise that can balance your mind, body, and spirit. I really didn't know much about yoga until I learned about it when studying for my master's degree. In learning about yoga, I wondered if it could really reduce stress? What I learned was that there are numerous studies that have shown that yoga can help many people better cope with stress[1] – something especially important to families of children with challenges.

There were two large studies that I remember. One study involved breast cancer survivors/patients and the other included caregivers for Alzheimer's patients. [2][3] Girlfriends, let's face it! Both of these groups have enormous, chronic stress. You really have to have some dedication day in and day out to care for a person with Alzheimer's disease. Also, battling and recovery from breast cancer ain't no walk in the park either. The studies showed that yoga helped both of these groups better cope with stress.

Girlfriend Story:

My girlfriend, Anna, was a single mom who adopted a little girl from Guatemala. After about two or so years she came to realize that her daughter was not at the same developmental level as her peers. Anna's daughter freaked out when she heard loud noises, especially a toilet flushing in a public space. She also had other non-typical reactions including being bothered by the tags in her clothes and the feel of her socks. Her daughter also preferred not to be touched or hugged, so Anna often felt rejected by her daughter. I sensed that Anna's daughter may have both sensory processing disorder challenges and possible attachment issues.

I told Anna about Carol Kranowitz's website, https://out-of-sync-child.com/, that described sensory processing disorder as well as sensory integration therapy, and suggested that she consider getting her daughter an evaluation from an occupational therapist. I also told her about my favorite book by Carol Kranowitz, *The Out-of-Sync Child Has Fun*, which has great techniques she could try at home with her child. Anyway, Anna did get her daughter evaluated and started therapy.

However, with the combination of her daughter's issues at school, the financial expense of treatment, and the greater demands on Anna's time running her daughter back and forth, Anna was feeling overwhelmed and stressed. She reached out to me and I asked her, "Did you ever try yoga?" Anna said that she had not. I told her that yoga is typically low cost and can be done in groups or at home. The "at home" option appealed to Anna, so she got herself a DVD and found out she liked yoga. Yoga helped Anna not only tone up her body but also better manage her stress. Anna now practices yoga at home a few days each week and can't live without it. She ranks it as important as her weekly latte.

Girlfriend Tips:

1. Give yoga a try

Not everyone loves yoga, but it is worth a try if you are interested. Many people really benefit from yoga. Girlfriends, it may not only reduce your stress but also tone those jiggly arms and thighs that have been bothering you.

2. Try different styles of yoga

There are many different styles of yoga. Some of the most common ones are the "Karma" and "Hatha" styles. Check out some online videos and see which one fits your fancy.

3. Make a schedule to do yoga

Many girlfriends like to do yoga first thing in the morning to set the stage for their day. Others prefer to do yoga in the evening. If you do yoga at home, it doesn't cost you anything. Also, when you are pressed for time, yoga can be done quickly so you don't have to break your schedule.

* * *

What I Wish I Would Have Known:

I wish I would have known how profound the benefits of yoga are for those who are subject to chronic stress. It really does help many people find the balance in their life that they have been searching for. I look at yoga as a three-for-one type of exercise because it can tone your body, balance your spirit, and calm your mind. What other exercise can do that for you?

IT'S A WRAP, NOW WHAT?

Thank you for reading this book. I hope you have found it helpful. I know I have thrown a lot of information at you and that you may be feeling overwhelmed. What should you do next? I recommend that you look at the table contents again and decide what issues are most relevant to your personal situation. I often find that starting with *"Respite Care"* for you and your family is a great place to begin. Respite care can help you get a break so that you can settle your mind to come up with a game plan, reset perspective and reduce stress. Also, *"Self-Compassion"* is another good chapter to reread and to practice the suggested exercises so you aren't so darn tough on yourself.

I wrote this book so that we girlfriends can learn from each other. As a parent of a child with challenges, we are not alone and face similar problems. Feel free to share with other girlfriends what you have learned from this book. I sincerely welcome that.

Although it is often not easy, we are super power women and can make a huge difference in our children's lives. We are girlfriends on a mission. Hang in there, girlfriends. We are there for each other.

If you have any questions or comments, please feel free to email me at Robin@SpecialChildWellness.com. Please put *"BOOK"* in the subject line.

My very best to you,

Robin

Robin Bartko

THANKS & ACKNOWLEDGMENTS

I want to thank some wonderful people who have helped me on my journey of life or with writing this book.

The Fam

Christina – for bringing joy in my life
Dennis – my dedicated partner in life that has helped me through both the good and tough times
Mary Beth – providing respite care when we were at wits end
Nick – my special angel
Noah – for teaching me so much about life and people

My Adoption Girlfriends

Your love & dedication is beyond words. You know who you are.

My Other Girlfriends

My shoulders to cry on and my friends to laugh with. You know who you are.

Dedicated professionals that I met through my adoption website

Dr. Lark Eshleman
Dr. Ronald S. Federici
Dr. Alla Gordina
Michelle Hughes
Dr. Jeri Jenista
Carol Stock Kranowitz
Dr. Todd Ochs
Inna Pecar
Dr. Thomas Phelan

My awesome professors and mentors from the Maryland University of Integrative Health

You were always willing to answer one more question ...

Sophia Kuziel
Liz Lipski PhD
Rebecca Pille PhD
Claudia Joy Wingo

END NOTES

Chapter 2: Stress Management 101

1. "Raising and Healing the Adopted Child." *PRWeb*, 8 May 2007, www.prweb.com/releases/2007/05/prweb524447.htm.

2. "Dr. Federici." *Dr. Federici*, www.drfederici.com/.

3. TEDtalksDirector. "How to Make Stress Your Friend | Kelly McGonigal." YouTube, YouTube, 4 Sept. 2013, www.youtube.com/watch?v=RcGyVTAoXEU.

Chapter 3: Communicating with Your Child and Significant Other

1. http://www.5lovelanguages.com/

2. "Clinical Psychology Internship." *School of Medicine Loma Linda University*, medicine.llu.edu/academics/resources/brain-based-techniques-retention-information.

Chapter 4: Fostering a Positive Relationship with Your Child

1. *Lark Eshleman, Ph.D.*, www.larkeshleman.com/.

Chapter 7: Celebrating the Good Stuff and Staying Positive!

1. Hanson, Rick. "Take in the Good." *Dr. Rick Hanson*, 29 July 2018, www.rickhanson.net/take-in-the-good/.

2. "How Complaining Rewires Your Brain for Negativity and Literally Kills You." *Learning Mind*, 16 Aug. 2018, www.learning-mind.com/complaining-brain-negativity/.

3. *Pretty Woman*. Directed by Gary Marshall. Performances by Richard Gere and Julia Roberts. Buena Vista Pictures, 1990.

Chapter 9: Managing School Issues

1. A 504 Plan is a plan developed by the school in cooperation with the parent(s) to "ensure that a child who has a disability identified under the law and is attending an elementary or secondary educational institution receives accommodations that will ensure their academic success and access to the learning environment." It differs from an Individualized Education Plan (IEP) in that it does not provide specialized instruction. [http://www.washington.edu/do it/what-difference-between-IEP-and-504-plan]

Chapter 11: Parent Training & Support

1. "Attention-Deficit / Hyperactivity Disorder (ADHD)." *Centers for Disease Control and Prevention*, Centers for Disease Control and Prevention, 19 Sept. 2018, www.cdc.gov/ncbddd/adhd/treatment.html.

Chapter 12: Finances

1. "Public Policy and Legal Advocacy." The Arc | Funding, www.thearc.org/what-we-do/public-policy/funding

Chapter 13: Self-Compassion

1. Neff, Kristin. "Self-Compassion." *Self-Compassion*, self-compassion.org/
2. Neff, Kristin. "Self-Compassion Exercises by Dr. Kristin Neff." Self-Compassion, self-compassion.org/category/exercises

Chapter 14: Meditation

1. Bloom, Deborah. "Instead of Detention, These Students Get Meditation." CNN, Cable News Network, 8 Nov. 2016, www.cnn.com/2016/11/04/health/meditation-in-schools-baltimore/index.html.

2. "Since 2003, MindUP, the Signature Program of The Goldie Hawn Foundation, Has Been Helping Children Develop the Mental Fitness Necessary to Thrive in School, Work and Life." *Visit Current MindUP.org*, mindup.org/.

3. "Welcome." *Your Skillful Means*, yourskillfulmeans.com/.

4. "Whole Health For Life." *Learn to Communicate Assertively at Work*, 11 Dec. 2017, www.va.gov/PATIENTCENTEREDCARE/Veteran-Handouts/Introduction_to_Mindful_Awareness.asp.

Chapter 15: Yoga

1. Diamond, L. (2012). The benefits of yoga in improving health. Primary Health Care, 22(2), 16-19. doi:10.7748/phc2012.03.22.2.16.c8961

2. Culos-Reed, S. N., Carlson, L. E., Daroux, L. M., & Hately-Aldous, S. (2006). A pilot study of yoga for breast cancer survivors: Physical and psychological benefits. Psycho-Oncology, 15(10), 891-897. doi:10.1002/pon.1021

3. Danucalov, M. A., Kozasa, E. H., Ribas, K. T., Galduróz, J. C., Garcia, M. C., Verreschi, I. T., . . . Leite, J. R. (2013). A Yoga and Compassion Meditation Program Reduces Stress in Familial Caregivers of Alzheimer's Disease Patients. Evidence-Based Complementary and Alternative Medicine, 2013, 1-8. doi:10.1155/2013/513149

www.ingramcontent.com/pod-product-compliance
Lightning Source LLC
Chambersburg PA
CBHW021208020426
42331CB00003B/265